Spain

Spain

MARTIN HOWARD

CHARTWELL
BOOKS, INC.

CHARTWELL BOOKS, INC.
A Division of
BOOK SALES, INC.
114 Northfield Avenue
Edison, New Jersey 08837

ISBN-13: 978-0-7858-2373-5
ISBN-10: 0-7858-2373-5

Cataloging-in-Publication data is available from the Library of Congress

Editor: Don Gulbrandsen
Design: Danny Gillespie/Compendium Design

Photography: The Publisher would like to thank the Spanish Tourist Office for providing the Tourspain photographs in this book, in particular Esther Rojo Barroso for her help in choosing the material.

Printed in China

Page 1: The island of Ibiza still has a number of watchtowers built as part of the island's defense system. This is the Torre de Can Pere Mosson, also called the tower of Balàfia, and is located near the town Sant Llorenç.

Page 2-3: The distinctive old windmills of Campo de Criptana, Castilla La Mancha.

Right: A vista of La Alhambra, the exquisite Moorish palace in Granada. The entire complex is surrounded by a fortified wall and the simple, graceful architecture belies the rich ornament and pleasure grounds to be found within.

Contents

Introduction: The History of Spain

Occupying roughly five sixths of the Iberian Peninsula and cut off from the rest of Europe by the Pyrenees, Spain has a unique and flamboyant personality that has been created by the weaving together of many colorful strands. More than any other European nation, it is a land of variety and contrast. Within its borders are snow-capped mountains and palm-fringed beaches, vast orange groves and arid deserts, cities crammed with architectural delights, and rural villages seemingly untouched for generations. Historically, too, Spain is a patchwork of influences. Throughout its early history Spain was invaded, conquered, and conquered again. While the official language is Castilian Spanish, many of the country's northern inhabitants prefer Catalan. In the Basque region Euskara remains a common tongue and the people of Galicia continue to speak Galician. In fact, Spain is a true "melting pot"—the Spanish can count among their ancestors Phoenicians, Celts, Greeks, Carthaginians, Romans, Jews, Visigoths, and Muslims and each culture has left something of its own stamp upon the Spanish way of life.

Indeed, it was not until the late fifteenth century that Spain's modern history as a unified kingdom began. The coming together of the two great kingdoms of Castile and Aragon, through the marriage of Ferdinand of Aragón and Isabella of Castile, provided the impetus for a dazzling ascent. Spain quickly became a crucible of art and literature as well as one of the world's most powerful seafaring nations. It was also the heart of a mighty empire, a legacy that can still be felt around the globe and in the Americas in particular. With an extraordinary cultural heritage that embraces some of the greatest artists—El Greco, Diego Velasquez, Francisco Goya, and Pablo Picasso—plus Gothic cathedrals and Gaudi's fantastical buildings, and a musical culture that owes much to Spain's invention of the guitar, Spain is a tapestry far more complex that the popular perceptions of bullfights and sangria.

In fact, it is thought that Spain was populated by tool-using hominids starting at an earlier date than anywhere else in Europe. The fossils found in the cave of Atapuerca, as well as stone tools unearthed around Soria and Madrid, suggest that *Homo erectus* arrived in the Iberian Peninsula about 800,000-1,000,000 years ago. Later—about 200,000 B.C.—Neanderthal man made an appearance, migrating from southern France into northern Iberia. They occupied the peninsula for tens of thousands of years until being slowly displaced by modern humans retreating from the Central Asian Steppes during the peak of the Ice Age around 40,000 B.C. Ten thousand years later these emigrants were followed by another wave of humans, a group to whom many of today's Spaniards and Portuguese can trace their genetic heritage. Vivid evidence of their artistic skill can be found at Altamira in northern Spain. The cave paintings here date to roughly 15,000 B.C. Discovered by a hunter—Modesto Cubillas—in 1868, the depictions of bison and other wildlife are so fresh in appearance and beautifully executed that experts refused for many years to believe they were genuine.

Hunting and gathering gave way to Neolithic farming around 5000 B.C. The following millennia saw the rise of first bronze and then iron technologies as well as the arrival of new migrants and the development of unique cultures among the indigenous peoples. The first newcomers on the scene, arriving around 3000 B.C., were Iberians (from farther east along the Mediterranean shore). They settled along the southern and southwestern seaboard.

Around 1100 B.C. the Phoenicians began to build trading ports along the south coast, including at Cádiz (then known as Gadir and thought to be the oldest extant city in western Europe) in 1104 B.C. It was the Phoenicians who gave the Iberian Peninsula its first taste of olive oil and wine; they also introduced iron to the region. Not far behind them were the Greeks and Carthaginians, who founded their own colonies on the Mediterranean shores.

The first wave of Celt migrants arrived in the ninth century B.C. and was followed two hundred years later by another. Originally settling in the north of the peninsula, the Celts slowly moved south and integrated with the Iberians who were moving north. Their meeting gave rise to the Celtiberian folk of the interior, people who married the metallurgic know-how of the Celts with the culture of the Iberians. Another notable people of this era include the Tartessians, now known to us through only a few literary references and a handful of artifacts. Their home was modern Andalusia and it appears that they were an advanced people, skillfully working in metal and traveling as far as Britain to trade.

What would eventually become Spain was, in fact, a dynamic and diverse place even before recorded history. It was about to be visited by another culture though, and one which did not intend to coexist in peaceful trade. To the east, the fortunes of Rome were rising.

The Second Punic War of 218–201 B.C. saw Rome pitted against the Cypriot-Phoenician colony of Carthage and its dependencies, among which were large swaths of the eastern seaboard of the Iberian Peninsula as well as the valley of the River Baetis. Because these lands provided the Carthaginians with fierce native troops as well as vast amounts of silver with which to finance their war efforts, Iberia was at the very center of the war. Even while the first campaigns were being fought in Italy, Roman troops were spreading along the Mediterranean coast of Spain. This first expedition succeeded in capturing the Carthaginian town of Sagantum in 211 B.C., but was later defeated at the Battle of the Upper Baetis. A second expedition, the following year, headed straight for Carthago Nova, effectively the Carthaginian capital in Iberia. The city fell after a

LEFT: Map showing the main geographical features of Spain.

OVER PAGE: Close to A Garda, on Mount Santa Tegra, are the remains of a settlement once populated by Spain's early Celtic immigrants. The site has incredible views, as well as a small museum.

short siege. By 206 B.C. Carthaginian Iberia was in the hands of the Romans, which was formalized in 201 B.C under the terms of the peace treaty after Roman victory. However, the Romans kept the name that Carthage had given its colony—Hispania.

For a large portion of the next two centuries, Hispania was torn by almost constant strife as first the Iberian tribes rebelled fiercely against Roman rule and then Roman struggled against Roman in civil war. Nevertheless, as the first century B.C. drew to a close Hispania, now divided into three provinces—Tarraconesis, Lusitania, and Baetica—had acquired all the hallmarks of a Roman territory, including ampitheaters, forums, temples, roads, viaducts, and, of course, taxation.

Existing towns were improved and new ones built, while under Roman tutelage Hispania became both prosperous and increasingly cosmopolitan. By A.D. 74 every town was given Latin status by Emperor Vespasian, granting Roman citizenship to the entire country. This act reflected the importance the Roman Empire attached to a country from which flowed enormous amounts of olive oil, wheat, and wine as well as iron, tin, silver, gold, and lead.

The Romans left much physical evidence of their rule in Spain. Important archeological sites include the vast Itálica, near Seville, the birthplace of Emperor Hadrian. Mérida (once capital of the Luisitania region) also has a wealth of remains, such as the Trajan archway, Circus Maximus, bridges, aqueducts, and the Temple of Diana. At Segovia can be found one of the most impressive extant examples of Roman aqueduct construction, still working after almost two thousand years. The remains of Roman buildings can be found throughout modern Spain, but perhaps the most significant, and lasting, Roman legacy is not a road, a theater or a town—no matter how impressive. Instead, Spain is indebted to the Romans for its Latin-derived language, as well as laying the foundations for its legal system and municipal government as well as the introduction of Christianity.

After six hundred years of Roman rule in Hispania, the empire's ability to protect its possession had become increasingly weak. The mighty empire had been split in two, reunified, and was under increasing military pressure, not least from Germanic tribes sweeping across Europe. In A.D. 409 the Suevi, Vandals, and Sarmatian Alans were forced from Gaul into Iberia by the advancing Visigoths. The Suevi occupied what is now northern Portugal and Galicia, while the Vandals and the Alans settled in the area that is traditionally believed to still bear their name: Andalusia.

Their stay was not to be a long one, but Rome's days were now numbered. Unable to flush the Germanic tribes from Hispania with his own forces, the western Roman Emperor, Honorius, tasked his new brother-in-law, the Romanised Visigothic King Athaulf to rid Hispania of them. In return, Athaulf was accorded settlement rights. By 429, the Visigoths had forced the Alans and Vandals into North Africa and the Suevi were defeated in 585. Now the Visigoths ruled almost the whole of Hispania from a court established in Toledo in 484. While they governed in the name of the emperor, the kings were all but autonomous, though they relied heavily on Roman institutions, and particularly the Roman Catholic Church, to administer the country.

The coexistence of the Roman infrastructure and Visigoth monarchy was always an uneasy one, even after Reccared, the Visigoth king, converted to Catholicism in 587. Hispania's new rulers held themselves aloof from the workings of their kingdom, to the extent that today there is little to mark the Visigoth period in Spanish history. Their armies comprised mostly of slaves and Visigoth nobles appear to have been primarily concerned with personal enrichment and fighting among themselves. The fearsome barbarian horde seemed content to simply let business go on as usual while they indulged in feuds, assassinations, and usurpations. This lack of interest in the state and its governance meant that where elsewhere in Europe the Roman way of life was almost completely overthrown, in Hispania it merely dwindled. With the country's administration weakened and its people bearing little or no loyalty to their rulers, the Visigoth's primacy provided an open invitation to foreign powers. Spain's next invaders would leave a much more lasting impression on the country.

In 711, the troops of Tariq ibn-Ziyad crossed the straits of Gibraltar from Muslim North Africa and defeated the Visigoth King Roderic at the Battle of Guadalete. More Muslim armies followed, and swept through Hispania. During a wildly successful military campaign, almost the whole of the Iberian Peninsula fell to the Muslims and further incursions into Europe were only halted by Charles Martel at the Battle of Tours in 732. The "Moors" as they were known (the word comes from the Latin name for Berber tribes in Mauretania, mauri), brought with them customs, science, religion, and culture that would set the Iberian Peninsula apart from the rest of Europe.

However, one small part of the country remained in Christian hands. Under a Visigoth noble named Pelayo, a small army in the north defeated the might of the Moors. Pelayo became the king of Asturias, and, as Christians migrated, the north of Spain would become increasingly powerful.

For the time being though, the Iberian Peninsula was under the rule of the Muslim invaders. Now named Al-Andalus, Moorish Spain became a part of the Caliph of Damascus, until Abd al Rahman I declared the independent Emirate of Córdoba in 756. Abd al Rahman III would pronounce it a Caliphate in its own right during the tenth century.

The first decades of Muslim rule were unsurprisingly rife with conflict between Christian and Muslim, but as the country settled under Abd al Rahman I, away from the constant battles in the north, Moorish Spain began to flourish. Old Roman irrigation was renewed and expanded and new crops were brought to the country—including oranges, lemons, apricots, peaches, figs, pomegranates, sugar cane, saffron, cotton, and rice—many of which are still at the heart of Spain's agriculture and help define its cuisine.

While agriculture was transformed, Al-Andalus also witnessed a scientific and artistic revolution, which would continue until late in the Moorish era. Mathematical innovations such as the astrolabe device transformed navigation and astronomy, and lavish mosques and palaces were constructed. Today, some of the finest examples of Moorish architecture can be seen in the south of Spain. Córdoba's Great Mosque, the Mezquita is a brilliant example of Islamic ornamentation, while Grenada's Alhambra is justly famous as a jewel of art and craftsmanship.

The north, though, from the earliest days of Muslim rule was a constant thorn in the side of the Moors. Around A.D. 825 a tomb was discovered near the Atlantic coast and was declared to be that of St. James (Santiago) by Bishop Teodomiro. The chapel that was built there would later become the imposing cathedral of Santiago de Compostela, but more importantly for the northern Christians of the ninth century, the saint's relics provided a banner to which they could flock. Declared the patron of his land by King Alphonse II (St. James is Spain's patron saint to this day), Santiago became known as "Matamoros" (the Moor Slayer) and helped bring together the internally warring Christian kingdoms of Spain's north.

Nevertheless, the Reconquista was still many years away. In the tenth century, Muslim armies under Al-Mansur attacked Christian lands, taking Santiago de Compostela itself in 997. The Christians' luck was about to turn though. After Al-Mansur died in 1010, Moorish Spain descended into civil war and was broken up into small kingdoms, or taifas. Gradually the northern Christian kingdoms expanded. Toledo was captured in 1085. As the Christian realms pushed southward, armies from the north of Africa were invited to help shore up Muslim power. The arrival of the Almoravids and Almohades spelled the end of the tolerant Islamic regime, and with the persecution of Christians and Jews the conflict between north and south became increasingly a holy war.

As the Reconquista gathered pace, distinct kingdoms developed in the north—León, Navarra, Catalonia Aragón, and Castile. Of these, the latter two were the most powerful, allied as they were with Portugal and France. In 1469, Princess Isabella of Castile and Prince Ferdinand of Aragón united in the most momentous marriage in Spain's history. Isabella became queen of Castile in 1474, and Ferdinand king of Aragón in 1479. Together Spain's monarchs brought almost all of the country under their rule and vanquished the remaining Muslim stronghold of Grenada, thus beginning Spain's modern history as a united country. (Navarra would be the final kingdom to be annexed in 1512). Spain was also to come together under one religion: Roman Catholicism. The Alhambra Decree of 1492 banished all Jews from the country and an inquisition was set up to ferret out those who had not made a sincere conversion. Unconverted Muslims were banished in 1502. By the time it was abolished in 1834, the Spanish Inquisition's task had expanded to persecute anybody found guilty of heresy (including Protestants) as well as sexual misdemeanors and witchcraft. About 5,000 people were executed and many more tortured, imprisoned, or fined.

In the same year that the Alhambra Decree was announced, Antonio de Nebrija published Grammar of the Castilian Language, completing the country's adoption of its own official language rather than Latin, while Isabella and Ferdinand made another momentous decision in sponsoring the Atlantic voyage of Italian Christopher Columbus. Forays into the New World would now begin to fill Spanish coffers and make the country a power to be reckoned with on the world stage.

Spain's empire grew quickly. Soon after Columbus's discovery, Spanish conquistadores began to pour into South America. In 1519, Mexico fell to Cortés while in 1532 a force of fewer than 180 foot-soldiers and cavalry under Pizarro overwhelmed Peruvian forces of 80,000 and the Incan Emperor Atahualpa was executed. Chile was subjugated by 1541. In fact, Spain's empire would become one of the largest in human history, stretching across the Americas, from what would become Canada to the bottom tip of South America. Along the way, the conquistadores destroyed entire civilizations.

To put Spain's dizzying ascent into context it is worth looking at the power wielded by Charles, the grandson of Isabella and Ferdinand, who had married their children off with meticulous political skill. Though his grandparents had begun their rule over a fractured Spain, parts of which were still under Muslim rule, Charles boasted the following among his titles: King Charles I of Spain; Sovereign of the Burgundian Netherlands; King of Naples and Sicily; Archduke of Austria; King of the Romans; Charles V Holy Roman Emperor; Count of Flanders; Duke of Brabant; Duke of Luxembourg; and Duke of Burgundy. Charles' lands stretched across Europe and, of course, he was also sovereign of Spain's vast overseas possessions. Although Charles split his empire in two on his abdication in 1556 (Spain, its New World possessions, and the Netherlands were given to Charles' son, Philip II, while the Holy Roman Empire and Austria were passed to his brother, Ferdinand), Spain was the supreme European power.

Charles I put the silver and gold that poured across the Atlantic to use in waging continual wars, particularly against France and the Ottoman Empire of Suleiman the Magnificent; these continued under his successors. Despite the military adventures of the sixteenth and seventeenth centuries that depleted Spain's enormous wealth as quickly as it was accumulated, the Habsburg dynasty of monarchs—of which Charles was the first—presided over a golden age of Spanish culture. Great artists such as El Greco and Velázquez were widely lauded, while writers and dramatists such as Miguel de Cervantes and Lope de Vega produced seminal works. Madrid became the Spanish capital in 1561 and its fabulous new buildings such as Felipe II's royal monastery, El Escorial, set new styles in architecture, while the Plaza Mayor (begun in 1619) hosted fantastic pageants and royal fiestas as well as executions. In 1580, Portugal was conquered by Spain, bringing the whole peninsula together for the first time.

During the seventeenth century Spain's preeminence began to slip. Economically drained by its financial support of the Roman Catholic forces during the Thirty Years War (1618–48), Spain's conflicts with France also continued. Portugal rebelled in 1640 and was joined by Catalonia. Although the latter was retaken in 1652, the interminable wars with France dragged on in the Netherlands, and a series of disastrous battles saw Spanish territories there fall to French forces. In fact, while the rest of Europe—particularly France and Great Britain—became increasingly dynamic and prosperous, Spain slumped under a king who was widely believed to have fallen victim to sorcery. While Charles II's many physical and mental disabilities (which included impotence and a tongue so large that few could understand his speech) can more likely be attributed to Habsburg inbreeding, he was not the vigorous monarch Spain needed to keep pace in modernizing Europe at the end of the seventeenth century. Two marriages failed to produce an heir and before he died, Charles named Philippe, Duke of Anjou and grandson of the reigning French monarch Louis XIV, as his successor, thus bringing the Bourbon dynasty to the throne. Almost immediately the European powers were plunged into a long running and damaging war.

At issue was the consolidation of French power in Spain, which was of grave concern to the other European nations. While Louis sought to assuage fears by decreeing that should Philippe ever ascend the French throne he would abdicate Spain's, his subsequent action in occupying remaining Spanish territories in the Netherlands sparked the War of Spanish Succession. Lasting from 1702 to 1713, the war spread to the Americas and eventually claimed more than 400,000 lives. Its resolution produced the Treaty of Utrecht, balancing the scales of power in Europe and reassigning Spanish holdings in North America and Europe. In forbidding the union of the Spanish and French monarchies, the treaty actually achieved a relatively modest amount more than Louis had already decreed before the war and most historians concur that a peaceful conclusion could have been reached diplomatically without the need for such a costly conflict.

Having finally been confirmed on the Spanish throne, Philippe V took his neglected and impoverished country into another confrontation almost immediately. In seeking to recover Sardinia and Sicily, which had been ceded to the Holy Roman Empire and Savoy respectively, Philippe goaded the other signatories of the Treaty of Utrecht into the War of the Quadruple Alliance, fought between 1718 and 1720. However, the alliance of European powers quickly gave Philippe an excellent demonstration of the decrepit state of his forces. Most famously, when the British captured a Spanish fleet at the Battle of Cape Passaro, they found the ships so decayed that they were deemed of no use whatsoever and destroyed.

Chastened, Philippe and his successors now showed more caution in foreign policy and concentrated on rebuilding the Spanish infrastructure. While the eighteenth century would be marked with numerous military actions, notably against the British in the Americas, these were now fought by better-equipped and better-organized forces. At home, taxes were lowered, new roads built, and the economy encouraged. The Spanish grip over its South American colonies was strengthened and trade became more efficient with the creation of the Honduras (1714), Caracas (1728), and Havana (1740) companies.

Bourbon reforms meant that the eighteenth century was a time of almost relentless growth for Spain, which peaked in the second half of the century following the horrors of the global Seven Years' War (1756–63). However, new prosperity was almost entirely due to trade with the Americas, and expanding mining operations there. Although the first signs of industrialization could be seen by the end of the century they were insignificant compared to Britain's and in the countryside the lives of most Spanish people were untouched despite

BELOW: An enchanting balcony amidst the palms on Gran Canaria.

LEFT: The Andalusian city of Cádiz is believed to be the oldest, continuously inhabited settlement in Europe, having been founded by the Phoenicians in 1100 B.C.

attempts to revolutionize agriculture. Culturally and artistically, though, Spain was changing dramatically. The strength of ties with France meant that Enlightenment ideas found a receptive Spanish audience—among the elite at least—while magnificent Baroque buildings were erected and Madrid transformed into an elegant and splendid city to rival Paris. Perhaps more importantly running water, a sewer system, and street lighting were installed.

As the nineteenth century approached, Spain had reversed the decay of the 1600s and again become a force to be reckoned with on the world stage. Although not yet equal in wealth and might to Britain and France, it was gaining rapidly. Unfortunately, history had yet another invasion in store, and this one would effectively end the nation's ambitions of empire.

The first swath of territory to be lost was the Louisiana Territory, a vast section of North America stretching from Canada to the economically significant port of New Orleans. Under Spanish control since 1763, the Spanish signed it over to France's new First Consul, Napoleon Bonaparte, in 1800. The treaty was made under duress and within three years Bonaparte had sold Louisiana to the United States. The next disaster for Spain came in 1805, when the British destroyed its main fleet, under French command, at the Battle of Trafalgar. In 1807, King Charles IV allowed French troops to cross Spain, ostensibly to reach Portugal, which had angered the now-emperor Napoleon by trading with the British. The subterfuge resulted in French forces occupying Spain's most important military positions. Bonaparte quickly consolidated. By 1808, Charles IV had been forced to abdicate and the French emperor's brother, Joseph, was placed on the Spanish throne.

Such was the ire of the Spanish people at the heavy-handed French conquest that they adopted a new form of fighting to combat their oppressors; it has been called guerrilla warfare ever since. Supported by British and Portuguese troops based in Portugal, the Spanish guerrillas weakened the French forces until the allied troops swept them across the Pyrenees in 1814.

Free again, Spain's problems had only just begun. As the first decades of the nineteenth century turned, its empire disintegrated. In many cases stirred into action by the passionate Simon Bolívar, country after country in South America rose up against their masters. Meanwhile, Spanish troops at home mutinied and had to be put down with the aid of troops from France. By 1825, Spain's vast empire in the New World had shrunk to just Cuba and Puerto Rico. By the end of the century these, too, would be gone.

Across the Atlantic, the vacuum created by the fallen monarchy and a desperate economic situation left Spain fragmented and at war with itself. The remainder of the nineteenth century saw civil conflict and revolution as the followers of rival monarchs Isabella II and Don Carlos fought over the throne, while liberals and republicans gathered support. The creation of the First Republic (1873) lasted only a year and a coup d'état soon put the Bourbons back on the throne. Isabella's son, Alfonso XII, worked hard to re-impose order on his country, but his reign was cut short by an early death in 1885 and Spain struggled to free itself from a growing cadre of anarchists.

The nineteenth century ended dramatically: In 1897 prime minister Cánovas del Castillo was murdered by anarchists and the following year saw Spain defeated in the Spanish-American war, which led to the loss of Cuba and the Philippines. This was a dreadful blow to Spanish pride and would give rise to a new breed of intellectuals and politicians calling ever more stridently for reform.

Despite a vibrant arts culture (Gaudí's first important work—Casa Vincens in Barcelona—dates to 1885 and Picasso founded the *Arte Joven* magazine in Madrid in 1901), as the twentieth century dawned, Spain found itself swamped by the same problems. Anarchy and fascism were on the rise, the labor unions increasingly powerful, and the country lagged far behind its European neighbors in industrialization. In 1912, anarchists assassinated another prime minister—José Canalejas—in Madrid. The country's fortunes rose briefly during World War I, however. Where elsewhere in Europe a generation of men were suffering horror and death on the battlefield, Spain remained neutral. By producing arms and supplies for both sides, the country experienced a much-needed boom. It was not to last though; with the war over the economy slowed once more and the misnamed Spanish Flu epidemic of 1918–19 decimated towns (the flu was a global epidemic and is thought to have originated in the United States).

An uprising in Spanish Morocco saw one of the few remaining outposts of empire achieve independence in 1921. In response, King Alfonso XIII lent royal support to the dictatorship of General Miguel Primo de Rivera who staged a coup d'état in 1923. For a few years the generally mild dictator brought some relief to Spain. Industry was encouraged, new public works begun, and the outline of a new constitution, which would give women the vote, drafted. Joining Spanish forces with French, the Moroccan territories were won back. De Rivera, it seemed, genuinely wished to reform Spain and then hand power to the people. In 1929 Barcelona and Seville staged superb exhibitions of art and industry. Nevertheless, Spain was—again—economically sickly and support for de Rivera had withered. He resigned in January 1930. Having backed the dictatorship for so long, Alfonso's reputation was also in tatters and he abdicated the following year. The Second Republic was created and instantly gripped by vicious political divisions. Violence and assassination blossomed in Spain, and administration slid into chaos. Civil war was inevitable.

The war began when General Francisco Franco landed from Morocco with his army in July 1936. Over the next three years Spain was devastated by a bitter conflict in which atrocity and massacre was commonplace. By April 1, 1939, the republic was finished and Franco victorious. The brutality that "el Generalísimo" delivered in response to any dissent—as well as his fascist sympathies—have tarnished Franco's legacy, but while he was a draconian authoritarian, Spain at last found stability under his rule and began to find its modern feet.

Officially neutral during World War II, Franco quietly aided the axis powers until it became obvious that events had turned against Hitler and Mussolini. Following the war, Spain was internationally isolated, but nevertheless began to advance significantly. The pace was quickened after the Pact of Madrid was signed with the United States in 1953. Fascists in Franco's administration were quietly replaced with technocrats intent on developing Spain's economy. Their success was outstanding and has since been called the "Spanish Miracle." From 1959 to 1973, Spain was second only to Japan as the fastest growing economy on Earth and the living conditions of its citizens increased in step. Industry boomed and Spain opened its doors to a new breed of tourists.

In 1947, Franco had pronounced Spain a monarchy without appointing a monarch to take the throne. In 1969, however, he named Prince Juan Carlos de Borbón as his successor. When Franco died in 1975, Spain saw a Bourbon king return to the throne. While the dictator was living, the king-in-waiting had stood quietly behind him, apparently endorsing Franco's policies. On his death, though, Juan Carlos immediately launched himself into transforming his country into a modern democracy, a project that is thought to have reached completion with the suppression of an attempted coup in 1981.

Modern Spain has sloughed off the problems that dogged the country for centuries. Indeed, by 1992 it was once again the center of the world's attention. The Olympic Summer Games were held in Barcelona, while Seville hosted EXPO '92, a hugely successful world exposition. Madrid was named the European Cultural Capital. Now a vigorous member of the European Union, Spain has adopted the Euro and has a well-developed industrial and agricultural economy as well as a thriving tourist industry.

While many of Spain's people now choose to live in cities, their parents and grandparents were mostly rural folk and strong links to the land and ancestral regions remain. Retaining its rich and colorful cultural heritage, Spain has embraced technology and innovation in the arts and sciences. Architects such as Santiago Calatrava and film directors including Pedro Almodóvar are acclaimed around the world. Having once expelled populations, Spain now welcomes more immigrants than any other country in Europe. Some hail from Spain's old territories, others from countries such as France and Britain that Spain once counted implacable enemies. Spain's home-grown citizenry has exploded, too, giving the country a dynamic population that is set to continue Spain's tradition of absorbing cultures into its own unique heritage.

RIGHT: A beautiful photograph showing the distinctive countryside of Castilla-La Mancha, familiar from Cervantes' classic tale *Don Quixote*.

A Timeline of Spanish History

1,000,000 B.C. Early hominids living on the Iberian Peninsula.

200,000-28,000 B.C. Spain is home to Neanderthals.

c. 40,000 B.C. First humans migrate into Spain.

c. 15,000 B.C. Altamira cave paintings created.

c. 5000 B.C. Agriculture begins.

c. 3000 B.C. Iberian colonists arrive.

c. 1100 B.C. Phoenicians begin to build trading ports on the Mediterranean coast.

c. 900 B.C. Celts begin to colonise northern Spain.

c. 600 B.C. Greeks begin to build trading posts on the Mediterranean shore.

400s B.C. Carthage becomes the primary Spanish power.

218 B.C. Second Punic War begins between Carthage and Rome

201 B.C. Second Punic War won by Rome. Spain becomes a Roman territory.

155 B.C. Portugal invaded by Romans

82-72 A.D. Roman Civil War. Pamplona founded by Pompey.

74 Rome grants Spanish citizens Latin status.

312 Christianity becomes the official religion under Emperor Constantine.

409 Vandals, Alans, and Suevi cross the Pyrenees.

415 Visigoths create a court at Barcelona.

429 Vandals and Alans driven from Spain.

585 Suevi tribes are defeated.

589 Visigoth King Reccared converts to Christianity.

711 North African Muslims arrive, defeat Visigoth forces at Guadalete and occupy the Visigoth capital of Toledo.

718 Visigoths establish a final stronghold in Asturias.

722 Christian forces under Pelayo resist the Moors at Covaonga.

732 Battle of Poitiers. Charles Martel stops the Moorish advance into France.

744 Forces of Asturian King Alfonso I conquer Léon.

756 Abd-ar-Rahman flees Syria and establishes Unayyad dynasty in Córdoba, which is declared an independent emirate.

785 Construction of Córdoba's Great Mosque begins.

822 Abd-al-Rahman II becomes ruler of Spain.

c. 825 A newly discovered tomb at Santiago de Compostela is proclaimed as that of St James.

905-925 Sancho I drives Moors from Pamplona.

c. 950 Léon forms an alliance with Castile.

976 Al Mansur overwhelms Barcelona.

997 Al Mansur takes Santiago de Compostela.

c. 1000 Abul Kasim writes the first surgical manual in Córdoba.

1013 Moorish Spain fragments into separate kingdoms, called taifas.

1035 Castile and Léon united through marriage of Fernando I of Castile to Sancha, sister of Bermudo III.

1085 Castile's Alfonso VI takes Toledo from the Moors.

1086 Almoravids arrive in Spain to help in the Moorish struggle against the Christian kingdoms.

1094 Rodrigo Díaz de Vivar, known as El Cid, takes Valencia.

1137 Catalonia and Aragon merged through marriage of Ramón Berenguer IV of Catalonia and Petronila of Aragón.

1143 Portugal recognized as a separate kingdom.

1147 Almohads arrive from North Africa.

1179 Kings of Castile and Aragón sign a treaty to cooperate in ridding Spain of the Moors.

1212 Battle of Las Navas de Tolosa. Christian forces defeat Almohads.

1230 Castile and Léon reunited under Fernando III.

1232 Kingdom of Grenada is created under Muhammad I.

1238 Construction of the Alhambra begins.

1469 Princess Isabella of Castile and Prince Ferdinand of Aragón marry.

1474 Isabella becomes queen of Castile.

1479 Ferdinand ascends throne of Aragón.

1480 Tomas de Terquemada becomes Spain's Grand Inquisitor.

1492 Grenada id defeated bringing all of Spain under Christian rule.

1492 About 160,000 Jews banished from Spain.

1492 Columbus lands in the New World.

1496 Ferdinand and Isabella's daughter, Joanna, marries Philip of Austria.

1512 Navarra is the last kingdom to be annexed.

1516 Charles I (Holy Roman Emperor Charles V) ascends Spanish throne.

1519 Ferdinand Magellan leaves Seville in an attempt to circumnavigate the globe.

1519 Mexico falls to Cortés.

1532 Peru conquered by Pizarro.

1554 Mary Tudor of England marries Philipe II.

1556 Charles I abdicates and divides his realms between his son and brother.

1561 Madrid is capital of Spain.

1563 Construction of the Escorial begins.

1580 Philip II moves an army into Portugal and claims the Portuguese throne.

1587 Spanish ships in Cadiz harbor destroyed by Francis Drake.

1588 Spanish Armada sails to England and is defeated.

1605 The first part of Don Quixote is published by Miguel de Cervantes.

1625 Diego Velazquez appointed court painter.

1640 Portugal and Catalonia rebel against Spanish rule.

1648 Treaty of Westphalia end the Thirty Years War and grants Holland independence.

1652 Catalonia retaken

1700 Charles II dies, leaving the throne to Bourbon Philippe of Anjou.

1702-13 War of Spanish Succession.

1718-20 War of the Quadruple Alliance.

1739-48 War of Jenkin's Ear between Spain and Britain is sparked by the report that a Spanish coast guard had cut off the ear of a British captain.

1756-63 Seven Years' War convulses Europe and the New World.

1786 Francisco de Goya becomes the court painter of Charles III.

1805 Spanish fleet defeated by Nelson at the Battle of Trafalgar.

1807 French army occupies Spain.

1808 Joseph Bonaparte takes the Spanish throne.

1808-14 The Peninsular War sees Portugal and Britain aiding Spanish guerrillas against the French.

1814 Ferdinand VII restored to the Spanish throne.

1824 Peru becomes the last South American country to gain independence.

1833-39 First Carlist war pits the followers of pretenders to the throne Isabella II and Don Carlos against each other.

1847-9 Second Carlist War

1870-75 Third Carlist War

1873 Spain's First Republic is declared, but only lasts one year.

1875 Isabella's son Alfonso XII ascends the throne, restoring the Bourbon line.

1885 Antoni Gaudî begins work on El Temple Expiatori de la Sagrada Familia in Barcelona.

1888 Universal Exhibition opens in Barcelona.

1894 Basque Nationalist Party founded.

1897 Anarchists assassinate Prime Minister Cánovas del Castillo.

1898 Philippines and Cuba win independence.

1912 Anarchists assassinate Prime Minister José Canalejas.

1921 Moroccans defeat the Spanish army and claim independence.

1923 A coup d'état sweeps Miguel Primo de Rivera into power.

1928 Salvador Dali and Luis Buñuel finish the surrealist movie Un Chien Andalou.

1930 De Rivera resigns.

1931 Alfonso XIII abdicates after republicans gain votes at local elections.

1936 General Francisco Franco declared head of state.

1936 Spanish Civil War begins.

1937 Basque town of Guernika is bombed by Nazi aircraft.

1937 Pablo Picasso unveils his painting, Guernica, at the Parisian World Fair.

1939 Nationalist forces take Madrid, ending the civil war and bringing Franc to power.

1947 Franco declares Spain a monarchy.

1953 Franco signs Pact of Madrid with the US, beginning of the end of Spain's international isolation.

1975 Franco dies, Bourbon Juan Carlos becomes King of Spain and head of state.

1977 First free elections held in Spain.

1986 Spain joins the European Community and NATO.

1992 Olympic Games held in Barcelona, Seville hosts Expo '92.

Northern Spain

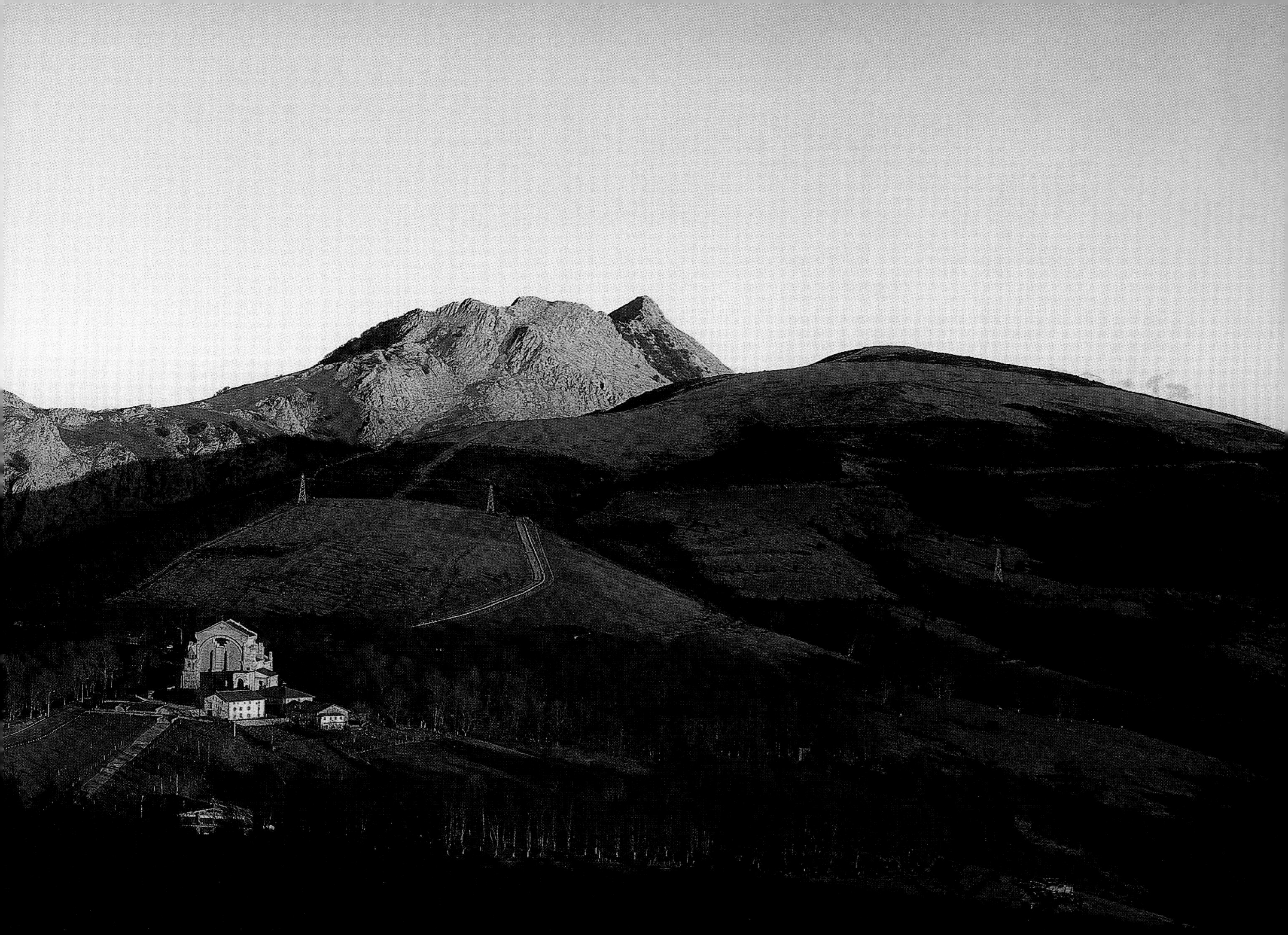

Northern Spain

Our journey around Spain begins with the regions of the north—Galicia, Asturias, Cantabria, Basque, La Rioja, and Navarra. Here, forested hills and mountains sweep down to the Atlantic coast where craggy cliffs are interspersed with quiet beaches. Lush valley meadows and river gorges characterise a part of the country that is less well-traveled than elsewhere in Spain, but which has a hoard of treasures: culture that stretches back to the cave paintings at Altamira; fine cuisine and viniculture; and a wealth of pre-Romanesque architecture in cities the Moors failed to grasp. Winding through a spectacular landscape dotted with untouched villages clinging to the sides of mountains are the roads along which pilgrims once made their way to pay homage to the relics of St. James in Santiago de Compostela.

Galicians trace their roots back to Celtic migrants of the ninth century B.C. and traces of Celtic culture are still visible in the region's art and audible in its music. Their language, too, is all its own. With the beautiful city of Santiago de Compostela at its heart, Galicia is a place largely untouched by the modern world. In the countryside steep farms are worked by oxen and fishermen still use traditional methods to land their catches. As you might expect from a region that has extensive coastline to the north, west, and south, Galician cuisine specializes in many superb seafood dishes.

To the east of Galicia is Asturias, the kingdom of Pelayo and site of his victory over the Moors in 722. This region nurtured its own culture while the rest of Spain was under Moorish dominion and today this can be seen in the beautiful old churches, particularly around its atmospheric capital, Oviedo. Here locals may speak Asturian or Eonavian alongside Castillian Spanish and old folkways and handicrafts are preserved in isolated mountain villages.

Separated from Asturias by the stately Picos de Europa massif, Cantabria, like its western neighbor, is a vertiginous and thickly forested region dotted with ancient villages and towns. East again, the Basque country (Euskadi in the local tongue), rolls down from the Pyrenees to the north east and is again proud of its difference from the rest of Spain. The most staunchly separatist of Spain's regions, most signs are in both languages and the people maintain their own culture, which includes some of the best cuisine to be found on the Iberian Peninsula. Scattered with sleepy villages, the Basque also has a glittering cultural and industrial center in Bilbao as well as sophisticated resorts, such as San Sabastián.

South from Basque is La Rioja, famous throughout he world for its wine, while to the west is Navarra, where the Basque culture also prevails. Perhaps most famous for the running of the bulls festival that takes place in its capital, Pamplona, Navarra has outstanding natural scenery (with no less than fifty natural preserves) and walled medieval towns.

PREVIOUS PAGE: The Urkiola mountain range in Biscay is formed by many limestone mounds. The highest mountain, Antobo, is 4,367 feet high.

LEFT: Donostia-San Sebastián became a popular Spanish beach resort after Queen Isabel II spent the summer there in 1845. In earlier centuries it had been a thriving port exporting wine and olive oil to France and England.

RIGHT: Inland Galicia boasts a fertile and mountainous landscape fretted with rivers and streams. The Ourense province has two national parks: the forests and meadows of Biaxa Limia-Serra do Xures and the more mountainous Monte O Invernadeiro.

Far left: Galicia's largest town, Vigo, has grown to become Spain's biggest fishing port, though now the harbor is as likely to welcome pleasure cruisers as it is fishing boats.

Left: Vigo's history centers on the old sailors' haunts by the port, but away from the atmospheric old bars the town is an attractively modern conurbation ringed by forested hills. It has a warm and sunny microclimate, as well as amenities such as the Campo de Golf shown here.

RIGHT: Once one of Christendom's most important places of pilgrimage, the cathedral in the heart of Santiago de Compostela houses the relics of St. James.

RIGHT: A view across Santiago de Compostela reveals the west façade of the cathedral. It stands on the site of the original structure, which was built during the reign of Alfonso II. Today's cathedral took about two hundred years to build, with construction beginning in the eleventh century.

HOTEL PUERTA
DEL CAMINO

LEFT: This statue of pilgrims marks the final leg of the Way of St. James. From here pilgrims are able to catch their first glimpse of the cathedral.

RIGHT: Santiago de Compostela continues to attract pilgrims and tourists as it did in medieval times. This photograph shows recently arrived pilgrims who have just walked the UNESCO-protected Way of St. James.

OVER PAGE LEFT: Galicia's second largest town, after Vigo, A Coruña is an elegant place of promenades, Romanesque churches, and graceful squares. An important seafaring town for centuries, A Coruña was the port from which the Spanish armada set sail for England in 1588.

OVER PAGE RIGHT: Perched on a promontory more than 300 feet high stands the octagonal tower of Cabo Vilan. A Coruña's lighthouse was one of the first to use electrical lights rather than candles. The town is also the home of the Torre de Hércules, a lighthouse originally built by the Romans and still working today. It was restored in the eighteenth century.

Previous pages: Forming a natural border between the two provinces of Lugo and Orense, the Canon del Sil is an enormous natural gorge surrounding the meandering flow of the River Sil. Some of the cliffs in this naturally imposing ravine are over 1,600 feet high.

Right: The Roman Bridge in Orense was one of the first built during the time of Augustus. Unfortunately, the bridge fell into disrepair but was reconstructed in the twelfth century using some of the original stones.

Far right: Nestled in the hilltops of an area affectionately called the birthplace of "Afiladores y paraguerios" (knife sharpeners and umbrella holders) stands the Santo Estevo de Rivas de Sil monstery. One of the region's oldest, it was originally established in the sixth century.

Left: Dating back to the third century, the Roman walls of Lugo were constructed as part of a defensive complex to protect the town from barbarian attack. UNESCO has declared them "a unique and exceptional example of Roman military fortifications."

Right: Padornelo is situated in the lush sloping fields of Lugo. This charming village contains the ancient church of "Hospitalarios de San Juan." Initially constructed in the fifteenth century, it now boasts a covered cemetery.

Over page left: Lugo is Galicia's largest province. Crossed by the Cantabrian mountain range with peaks up to 6,000 feet, fertile valleys where farming goes on as it has for centuries can also be found. Indeed, it is not unusual to see plows being pulled by oxen.

Over page right: The Asturian town of Cangas de Narcea lies on the confluence of the Narcea and Luiña rivers and can trace its roots back to pre-Roman times. Among its historic buildings are the monastery of San Juan de Corias and a Roman bridge.

BAR
VILLA DEL NARCEA
ANTONIO
EL REGALO

PREVIOUS PAGE LEFT: Asturias' Costa Verde is a stretch of rugged Atlantic coastline in the northwest part of the region that is interrupted by coves and picturesque fishing villages, such as Cudillero, shown in the photograph.

PREVIOUS PAGE RIGHT: To the south of Asturias are the crags of the Somiedo Nature Park, a UNESCO Biosphere Reserve since 2000. Noted for its abundant flora and fauna, the park is home to numerous species, including brown bears and wolves.

FAR LEFT: A back street in Oviedo, the capital of the Principality of Asturias. The city also contains a university founded in the early seventeenth century.

LEFT: The cathedral of San Salvador in Oviedo was built on the site of an earlier building in 1388 but was not completed until the sixteenth century by which time it had incorporated a mixture of architectural styles—although the principal effect is late gothic.

RIGHT: Roughly in the center of the Asturian coastline, just west of Gijón, are the stunning Armoricana quartzite rocks of Cabo de Peñas.

FAR RIGHT: Gijón itself was once an important Roman city and is still central to the region's economy. Though it has become a modern, industrial city, Gijón has sought to conserve its rich history and is today a sophisticated city of museums, archeological sites, and beautiful architecture. The photograph shows the old port.

LEFT: Among Gijón's many attractions are superb beaches, Roman baths, and festivals. The Baroque Palacio de Revillagigedo, shown here, is home to some important pieces of modern art and holds frequent festivals.

RIGHT: Further east along the coast from Gijón is the beautiful fishing village of Lastres. Visitors here often climb the cliffs to the Sanctuary of San Roque in order to take in the magnificent views of the Asturian coast.

FAR LEFT: Further along Spain's northern coast, in Cantabria, is the town of San Vincente de la Barquera. With the Picos de Europa mountains providing a dramatic backdrop, the town has atmospheric arcades and ramparts and some fine Romanesque architecture.

LEFT: The capital of Cantabria—Santander—is a beautiful coastal city with a long history. The cathedral marks the hilltop site where the Romans originally founded the city and dates back to the thirteenth century, though it was largely rebuilt after fire ravaged the city in 1941.

Left: Beyond the city itself is the elegant El Sardinero district and the Faro de Santander. Perched on dramatic cliffs, the lighthouse looks over some of the city's superb beaches.

ABOVE: Once the Basque region's only university, this impressive Renaissance building in Oñati dates to the mid-sixteenth century.

OVER PAGE: The Basque's Basílica de San Ignacio commemorates Saint Ignatius, who founded the Jesuit order. The grand seventeenth century structure encloses the original manor house where the saint was born and spent much of his early life.

RIGHT: Popular with surfers Playa de Laga on the Basque's Costa Vasca is typical of the region's rocky coastline, where wooded cliffs are punctuated by coves and beaches.

FAR RIGHT: The peaceful coastal town of Guernica was established in 1366 by Count Tello, who hoped to profit from its advantageous position, situated on two major roads and a port. However, the estuary on which it sits contains more Roman remains than any other site in Basque country, some dating as far back as 4 B.C.

Left: The ancient Oak of Gernika, or Gernikako Arbola, is a carefully protected 300-year-old petrified oak trunk under which the Kings of Castille promised to respect the freedom of the Basque people. This tree is one of the famous oaks many descendents.

Right: Emerging from the Cave of Santimamine, visitors can witness the magical sight of the Bosque de Oma. The pine trees have been decorated with partial paintings by the artist Agustin Ibarrola so that the complete pictures can only be seen from certain positions.

LEFT: The Paseo Campo de Volantin, also known locally as the "Zubizuri" (meaning "white bridge" in Euskera), was designed by Santiago Calatrava and was completed in 1997.

RIGHT: The largest Basque city, Bilbao, is surrounded by barren hills and its suburbs and industrial sites stretch out into the surrounding countryside for eight miles—but the true heart of the city is here in the medieval center. The winding alleyways are alive with the sound of music and tempting aromas from the many tapas bars.

OVER PAGE: The picturesque town of Errezil sits nestled in lush valleys of the Gipuzkoa province. With an area of only 764 square miles, it is the smallest province in Spain.

Left: The sleepy medieval town of Laguardia is the capital of the La Rioija Alavesa region where Rioja wine is made. The rich deep red wine has been produced here for centuries and tastings are readily available in the many wine cellars (or bodegas) throughout the town.

Over page: The elegant and sophisticated resort of San Sebastian has been popular with the aristocracy since the nineteenth century. Nowadays it is more of a family retreat but still boasts one of Spain's most luxurious hotels, the Maria Cristina.

FAR LEFT: This beautiful Gothic cathedral is situated in the old quarter of La Rioja's capital, Logroño, close to the Rio Ebro.

LEFT: Construction of the church of San Pedro de la Rúa began in the twelfth century and lasted until the sixteenth century. Reflecting many of the architectural styles that held sway during the four centuries of its construction, the church today towers over Estella from its perch on top of a cliff.

RIGHT: Logroño itself was once an important staging post on the pilgrim's route to Santiago de Compostela as well as the site of the Basque witch trials that began in 1609. Eventually over 7,000 cases were heard, making it the largest trial of its kind in history. This photograph shows the town's plaza.

LEFT: Estella, in Navarra, is another town that once would have bustled with pilgrims making their way to Santiago de Compostela. This bridge across the Rio Egea led them to worship at the Iglesia de San Pedro de la Rúa at the edge of the town.

RIGHT: Pamplona's cathedral is a Gothic masterpiece. Mainly built during the fifteenth century, it is just inside the city walls and contains the tombs of Carlos III and Queen Leonor.

ABOVE: The village of Arrízala in the Basque province of Avala contains the Paleolithic Dolmen de Sorginetxe.

OVER PAGE LEFT: The view across the Plaza del Castillo from Pamplona's Palacio del Gobierno de Navarra. The palacio is the home of Navarra's government and lies in the heart of the city.

OVER PAGE RIGHT: Old Navarra can still be found in the isolated Roncal valley. Here local farmers cultivate using traditional methods and produce some of the country's finest cheese.

RIGHT: Dominating the surrounding plain and also in the province of Alava, is the hilltop town of Laguardia. This region produces the famous Rioja wines

BAR IRUÑA

Eastern Spain

Eastern Spain

Eastern Spain is home to some of the world's most popular beaches along the Mediterranean coasts of Catalonia and Valencia, but away from the sea and sand are gems of scenery and heritage. In Barcelona, eastern Spain also has one of the world's most beautiful and culturally significant cities.

Aragón is sparsely populated, but rich in agriculture. Its landscape descends from the lake strewn Pyrenees in the north to plains of the Ebro Valley. Once an important provider of crops to Rome, many Roman ruins can still be found here while in isolated valleys are small communities that still speak the old Aragonese language.

Away from the beaches of the Costa Brava, Catalonia boasts a bewildering array of landscapes, including peaks that attract skiers. Just over thirty miles inland from Barcelona is the breathtaking mountain of Monserrat (which translates as "jagged mountain") with its medieval Benedictine monastery. While the "Spanish Miracle" of the 1970s has transformed some coastal areas into sprawling resorts, charming untouched fishing villages can also be found up and down the coast, along with peaceful coves of golden sand ringed by pine trees. Catalonia also has numerous UNESCO World Heritage Sites, among them the architectural works of Anton Gaudí in Barcelona. A city like no other, Barcelona is brimming with architectural wonders from every period, but is particularly rich in Modern works that give this creative and vital city a unique personality.

South of Catalonia, Spain's landscape changes again as the orange and lemon groves of Valencia unfurl. Here, the marks left by the Moors can be seen more plainly. Indeed, many local people still preferring to speak a language derived from the Moor colonists. Like its northern neighbor, Valencia's beaches attract holiday makers from far and wide, but outside the high-rise resorts such as Alicante and Benidorm are nature reserves, such as L'Albufera's freshwater lagoon, unspoiled towns and the bustling city including Valencia itself. Spain's third largest metropolis is a city of splendid architecture, colorful fiestas and

relaxed outdoor living, dominated by a thirteenth century cathedral.

South again is the small region of Murcia, which can trace its history back to the Iberians who gave their name to the peninsula and has long benefited from irrigation systems devised by the Romans and improved by the Moors. Murcia's second city, Cartagena began as the Carthaginian port of Cartago Nova. The interior of the region offers startling changes in landscape from desert to lush irrigated fields of flowers and vegetables while the coast is punctuated by seemingly endless beaches. Beneath the ground, Murcia also has vast cave systems.

PREVIOUS PAGE: Aragón's Parque Nacional de Ordesa y Monte Perdido contains some of Spain's most stunning scenery. Snow-capped peaks tower over lush forests and glacial canyons streaked with waterfalls.

FAR LEFT: Surrounded by the Pyrenees, the town of Panticosa lies in Aragón's Tena valley in the Huesca province, close to the French border.

LEFT: In the foothills of the Pyrenees, the village of Berdún sits atop a hill commanding sweeping vistas down the Aragón river valley. A fortress since Celtic times, it was later a thriving Roman town and still retains a timeless charm.

LEFT: Panticosa has a Romanesque church dating to the thirteenth century at its heart. It is now a successful ski and mountain sport resort with luxury hotels, spas, and casinos.

RIGHT: The original capital of Aragón, Jaca dates back to Roman times and is another of the region's unspoiled gems. The old streets around the cathedral area are particularly attractive.

RIGHT: About fifty miles from the city of Huesca, the village of Santa Cruz de la Serós is popular among tourists for the superb Romanesque architecture of its two churches.

FAR RIGHT: The Palacio de la Aljaferia in Zaragoza is a fortified palace that once served as the home of the Banu Hud family when Spain was under Moorish rule. Dating back to the eleventh century, it provided the composer Giuseppe Verdi with a setting for his opera *Il Travatore* and is now the seat of government for Aragón.

LEFT: Seen here across the Ebro River at dusk, Zaragoza is one of Spain's most historic towns, with a history stretching back to the time of the first Iberian migrants. The building with the four spires across the bridge is the Basílica de Nuestra Señora del Pilar, consecrated to the Holy Virgin of Pilar who is the patroness of all Spanish-speaking countries.

LEFT: Partially carved from the rock, the monastery of San Juan de la Peña is a unique national monument and believed to be the oldest monastery in Spain. It is located southwest of Jaca.

TIBUR HOTEL
GOYA

LEFT: Zaragoza's Plaza de Las Catedrales overlooked by La Seo cathedral. Aragón's capital city is rich in statues and monuments—as you might expect from a city that can trace its history back more than 2,000 years. Among its most important sites are Roman baths and a theater as well as the Don Pedro de Luna palace. The city is also home to many culturally significant museums.

RIGHT: The Parque Nacional de Ordesa was founded in 1918 and has since grown to cover more than 56,000 acres populated by many species of plant and animal life, including the ibex and the rare lammergeier, or bearded vulture.

PREVIOUS PAGE LEFT: About seventy miles south of Barcelona in the region of Catalonia is the city of Tarragona. Overlooking the Mediterranean are some of the finest Roman ruins in Spain, they have been designated a UNESCO World Heritage site. In Roman times the city was known as Tarraco and was the capital of the Hispania Tarraconensis region.

PREVIOUS PAGE RIGHT: One of Europe's biggest and best preserved Cistercian monasteries, the Monasterio de Santes Creus near Tarragona dates back to 1168.

RIGHT: Fifty miles northwest of Barcelona is the imposing Romanesque Cardona Colegiata, which dates to the eleventh century. It stands on the site of a previous structure that is believed to have been built in the fourth century.

FAR RIGHT: The coastal resort town of Sitges has long had a Bohemian reputation. For many years during the Franco era it was a center of counterculture and today the beautiful town hosts art and film festivals and is a popular destination for gay travelers.

LEFT: Designed by Antoni Gaudí, La Sagrada Familia in Barcelona is one of the world's most famous basilicas. Started in 1882 and still unfinished, Gaudí spent forty years working on the project.

ABOVE: Towering 180 feet over Barcelona, the Monumento a Colón commemorates Christopher Columbus. Tourists can climb to just below the great explorer's feet and look out over the city.

RIGHT: Plaza de Catalunya is considered Barcelona's central point and is popular with visitors. Surrounded by department stores and cafés, the plaza is endowed with fountains, sculptures, and grassy verges.

HOTEL BARCELONA

taxi

Far left: Another of Gaudí's triumphs in Barcelona is Casa Milà. Built between 1905 and 1907 in the Eixample district it is a testament to Gaudí's genius and paved the way for many other architects of the twentieth century to experiment with form and eccentricity.

Left: Parque de la Ciudadela was laid out at the end of the nineteenth century and occupies the site of Barcelona's old citadel. Beautifully designed and stocked with specimen trees and plants, it also has graceful fountains and sculptures by local Catalan artists.

Over page left: Since the 1992 Olympics, Barcelona has developed old waterfront areas that were previously industrial and replaced them with modern apartment buildings, marinas, waterfront promenades, and shopping malls.

Over page right: Barcelona's famous Manzana de la Discordia (Block of Discord) is a row of five buildings, each built by a different architect and each radically different in style. To the left of the photograph is the Ametller House, designed by Puig i Cadafalch and to the right Gaudí's Batlló House.

LEFT: Barcelona's early twentieth century architectural heritage also includes the superb Casa Lleo Morera, built in 1906 by Doménech i Montaner in the Art Nouveau style. It stands on the corner of Carrer del Consell de Cent.

RIGHT: The cloisters of Barcelona's beautiful Gothic cathedral are home to a fountain and small garden. Begun in 1298, the cathedral was not completed until the end of the nineteenth century.

LEFT ABOVE AND BELOW: Barcelona is famous for its festivals and carnivals, which attract performers and visitors from across the world. Although many have an international flavor, they continue to incorporate Spanish acts and traditions.

RIGHT: Just outside the bustle of Barcelona is Montserrat, which translates as "jagged mountain." Formed from pink conglomerate, the mountain is a dramatic landmark upon the slopes of which can be found the Benedictine abbey of Santa María de Montserrat, which some believe to be the resting place of the Holy Grail.

Left: Rising above Barcelona is the hill of Montjuïc, site of the 1929 International Fair and now replete with museums, galleries, fountains, and gardens. The Palacio Nacional, shown here, now houses a significant collection of medieval art.

Right: In the hills to the northeast of Barcelona is the charming medieval village of Rupit. Its cool forests and beautiful river make it a favorite destination for campers.

Over page left: Catalonian beaches are justly famous. This photograph shows the beach of San Pol de Mar, one of the region's quieter resorts which has grown up around an old Benedictine monastery.

Over page right: Once the capital of the county of Besalú, under the wonderfully named Wilfred the Hairy who united Catalonia, the town of Besalú is now a historical national property. Located in the northeast part of the region, its twelfth century Romanesque bridge is just one of the town's historic points of interest.

LEFT: Hidden in the Desierto Les Palmas (or Desert of the Palms) lies the ruins of a ancient Carmelite monastery. Originally built between 1697 and 1783, the building suffered severe damage following a number of earthquakes. A new monastery was built nearby, but the original remains a place of quiet contemplation and beauty.

LEFT: The former fishing village of Palamós has lain along the Costa Brava (meaning "wild coast") since the twelfth century. Now the village's main industry is tourism and it boasts white sandy beaches, sunlit coves, and sailing.

RIGHT: Standing over the picturesque town of Pals is the Torre de les Hores. This Romanesque tower dates back to the eleventh and thirteenth centuries and is rumored to be haunted by the ghost of Maria Can Pals, a medieval witch.

RIGHT: An ally of Rome in 219 B.C. the town of Sagunto was attacked by Hannibal. It is said many inhabitants threw themselves onto fires, rather than face the vengeance of Hannibal's men. The ruins of the Castillo de Sagunto and its fortifications run along the crest of a hill next to the modern-day town.

LEFT: In the heart of Valencia stand the four ultramodern buildings which together form the Ciutat de les Arts i de les Ciencies. Looking like a large blinking eye, L'Hermisferic, contains an IMAX cinema and planetarium.

LEFT: Built between 1482 and 1498, the wonderfully Gothic hall of La Lonja began life as an early stock exchange. Nowadays the vaulted ceilings are put to a more refined use and La Lonja has became a cultural center.

RIGHT: An eclectic mix of Romanesque, Gothic, and Baroque styles, Valencia Cathedral was first built in 1262 but has had several additions over the centuries. A chapel inside the cathedral holds a jeweled cup that is alleged to be the Holy Grail.

RIGHT: High on a hilltop in the Alicante region on the Costa Blanca is the small medieval town of Polop. Surrounded by lemon groves and terracotta-colored mountains, the simple beauty of the town inspired local author, Gabriel Miro, to write a story based in Polop.

Left: L'Umbacle in the Arts and Science Museum of Valencia is a long open archway dedicated to the study of botany. L'Umbracle contains thousands of different species of plants and flowers, all specifically chosen so that the forms and color change in tune with the seasons.

Right: Castillo de Santa Barbara was built on the summit of Mount Benacantil in the sixteenth century and offers a view of the entire city of Alicante.

LEFT: The pretty seaside town of Altea has kept much of its old world charm, unlike many neighboring towns in the vicinity of Benidorm. The village stands on a hill, a mass of white washed houses and winding alleyways, dominated by the blue tiled domes of the church.

RIGHT: The Valencian town of Biar boasts a walled castle, standing on top of a nearby hill. Biar is situated at the foot of the Sierra de Mariola, a mountain range and national park.

LEFT: The stunning seaside coves of Xabia in Alicante were once exploited by local pirates and smugglers. The many cliffs, caves and rocky islands made it an ideal place to hide.

RIGHT: In the Huerto del Cura (the Orchard of Hura) near the city of Elx, there are more than 140,000 square feet of lush garden, including 1,000 palms. Pictured is the Imperial Palm, a tree with a trunk split into eight branches.

FAR RIGHT: Elx is almost surrounded by a forest of palms, numbering more than 300,000. It is believed that the plants' ancestors were planted by Phoenician settlers around 300 B.C. The Elche Palm Grove became a World Heritage Site in 2000.

LEFT: South of Valencia is its smaller neighbor, Murcia. The town of Caravaca close to the western border has numerous old churches as well as a castle containing the Santuario de Vera Cruz, or sanctuary of the true cross, where a miraculous cross is said to have materialized in 1231.

LEFT: Murcia's capital is the town from which the region takes its name. Built on an inland plain, the city is one of the largest in Spain and was founded by the Moors with the benefit of a complex irrigation system. Today it is brimming with architectural and cultural delights, including its great cathedral, a casino that dates to 1847, and the Teatro de Roma.

RIGHT: Tarragona has been known as Imperial Tarraco since the Romans dominated the area and used the city as their regional capital. The region still contains some of the best preserved Roman remains in all of Spain.

FAR RIGHT: Iglesia de Santa María de Arties is one of many enchanting small churches built in the Catalan style in the Val d'Aran.

Central Spain

Central Spain

Comprising the four provinces of Castilla-La Mancha, Madrid, Extremadura (also spelt Estremadura), and Castilla y Leon, central Spain is a dramatic region of strong flavors, extreme weather conditions, and rich aromatic food and wine. Madrid, more than anywhere else in Spain, is renowned for its diverse climate, which is summed up neatly in the local saying, "Nine months of winter, three months of Hell."

Spain's capital since 1561, Madrid is situated almost at the geographical center of the country. Due to its inland location and relatively high altitude, the city experiences boiling hot summers and freezing winters. Madrid itself is split into several sectors, each with its own distinct atmosphere.

Old Madrid, on the western side of the city, encapsulates the ancient heart and history of the capital. The Inquisition held trials and carried out executions in the central Plaza Mayor—sometimes in the presence of the monarchy. Nowadays the once infamous site is filled with fashionable cafés and gift shops. There is also the Colegiata de San Isidro, Madrid's primary cathedral from the seventeenth century until 1993, when the Catedral de la Almudena was finally completed after a century of construction.

To the east of capital is "the Meadow" more commonly known as Bourbon Madrid. Once a tranquil garden district, this area has undergone considerable improvement thanks to the efforts of the Bourbon kings during the eighteenth century. This section now has lavish plazas, triumphal arches, and some of the best museums in all of Spain. Surrounding the busy metropolis is the calmer Madrid Province, a haven for commuters and tourists alike, offering great scenery and relief from the torrid weather of the city.

The arid plains of Castilla y Leon are filled with fine examples of ancient castles. During the tenth and eleventh centuries the area was a theater of war between the Moors and the Christians. Many villages were fortified against the battles that raged around them, but the best-preserved fortresses were

PREVIOUS PAGE: A few miles north-west of Sigüenza, Atienza is a medieval fortified town watched over by a ruined castle. This photograph shows the arcades of the Plaza del Trigo and the Iglesia de Santa María, which has an impressive collection of religious art.

LEFT AND BELOW: The landscape of Castilla-La Mancha today looks much as it would have done to Cervantes, whose *Don Quixote* immortalized the region in print. Its ochre plains and bare hills are punctuated still by windmills and ancient castles.

homes for the conquering nobility, such as the Alcazar in Segovia or La Moto castle in Medina.

Castilla-La Mancha is often associated with the story of Don Quixote and the empty plains spotted with windmills are extremely evocative of Cervantes' epic tale. There is more to this region than expansive plains: Castilla-La Mancha has two stunning National Parks and the world's largest stretch of vineyards.

Extremadura is a section of Spain seemingly untouched by modern life. Ideal opportunities await those who wish to discover a Spain thought long gone. Because of its remoteness, many fine examples of Roman architecture have passed unscathed through the centuries. In fact, very few of the towns or villages seem to have changed in decades.

Left: The bridge over the Rio Tajo—also called the River Tagus—near Toledo. It is the longest river on the Iberian peninsula and runs through from east of Madrid westwards through Spain to Portugal, where it enters the Atlantic Ocean at Lisbon.

Right: Rising above the River Targus is the old Visigothic capital of Toledo, a city that is redolent of history, not least in its narrow, cobbled alleys.

LEFT: A view over Toledo. On the right, the squat building with towers at each corner is the Alcázar, originally built as a palatial fort for Charles V and reduced to rubble during the Spanish Civil War. Now rebuilt, it contains the preserved headquarters of the Nationalists who withstood a seventy-day siege here.

RIGHT: One of the world's largest, Toledo's Roman Catholic cathedral stands on the site of a Visigoth church and Moorish mosque. Containing amazing works of art and sculpture—including El Greco's *The Denuding of Christ*—the cathedral was begun in 1226 and not finished until 1493.

LEFT: The graceful Church of Cristo de la Luz in Toldeo was built in 999-1000 as the Mosque of Bab Mardum. It was converted to a Christian place of worship after the conquest of Toledo in 1085.

RIGHT: The Puente del Arzobispo crosses the River Tagus near Toledo and was an important location during the Peninsula Wars.

DE NTRA SRA LA VIRGEN DE BIEN

LEFT: Beautiful examples of the work of Talavera de la Reina's ceramic workers can be found throughout the town, including here at the hermitage of Nuestra Señora.

RIGHT: The façade of Talavera de la Reina's Teatro Victoria decorated with the ceramic tiles for which the town is famous.

OVER PAGE LEFT AND RIGHT: Noted for its simple unadorned style, which set a new architectural trend in Spain, El Escorial in Madrid province was built between 1563 and 1584 as Filipe II's palatial retreat. While the building was intended as a place of peaceful contemplation, it houses an incredible wealth of artworks.

PREVIOUS PAGE LEFT: Madrid's Palacio Real is the official residence of the King of Spain, though it is actually used only for official engagements, the king preferring to live elsewhere. Building work began in 1734 after fire destroyed the fortress that previously stood on the site.

PREVIOUS PAGE RIGHT: Plaza de Cibeles is widely thought to be the most beautiful of Madrid's many squares; at its center is a fountain honoring Cibeles, the Roman goddess of nature. The square is edged by many impressive buildings, such as the Palacio de Comunicaciones seen here.

RIGHT: Another of Madrid's grand statues is the Fuente de Apolo in the Plaza Cánovas del Castillo. It dates to the early eighteenth century.

FAR RIGHT: Opened by King Juan Carlos and Queen Sofia in 1992, the Museo Nacional Centro de Arte Reina Sofia in Madrid is the nation's foremost center of contemporary design and modern art.

Left: In northeast Castilla y León is the charming city of Burgos, which can trace its roots back to a Celtiberian settlement of pre-Roman times.

Right: Burgos' cathedral is the third largest in Spain; it dates to 1221. One of the world's great Gothic cathedrals, it is richly ornamented with art statuary and detailed reliefs.

OVER PAGE LEFT: In the southeastern part of Burgos province are pine groves, rocky hills, and glacial lakes. The landscape is strewn with fossils as well as the marks of human history, such as hermitages and the ancient necropolis shown in the photograph.

OVER PAGE RIGHT: Once an important stronghold during the fight against the Moors, Frias Castillo occupies a commanding position over the town. Its distinctive tower is built into a rock known locally as "the tooth."

RIGHT: In the popular imagination, the central regions of Spain are sun-drenched and scorched, but winter can transform the landscape as this photograph taken outside Burgos shows.

RIGHT: The northern reaches of Castilla y León share a similar landscape with the regions to the north. Forested mountains latticed with rushing streams make it a very attractive area.

FAR RIGHT: Segovia in Castilla y León contains the highest concentration of Romanesque churches in Europe. The city's distinguishing landmark is the sixteenth century cathedral, known locally as Dama de las Catedrales.

LEFT: A dramatic photograph of Segovia in Castilla y León. The city's old quarter is built upon a rocky hill and is a treasure trove of history set in atmospheric cobbled streets.

RIGHT: At the heart of the Castilla y León region, the town of Palencia has more than fifty well-preserved Romanesque buildings that date to the time when the town was a cultural hub. It was here, in 1208, that the first Spanish university was founded. The photograph shows the church of San Martin Fromista.

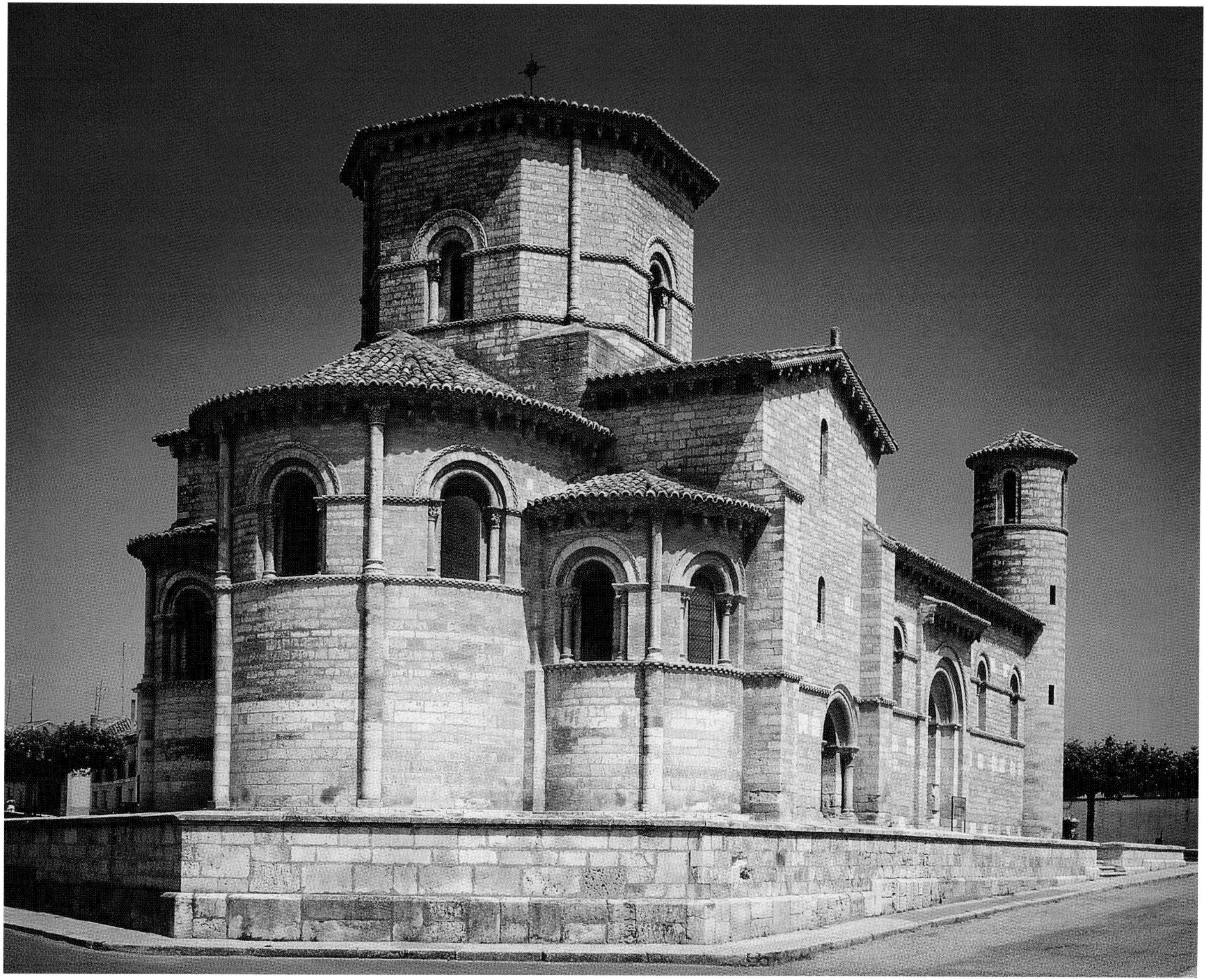

RIGHT: Seen here illuminated at night, the medieval walls of Ávila have encircled the oldest part of the city since the twelfth century and are amazingly well preserved.

ABOVE: Ávila's walls are a little more than a mile long and incorporate eighty-eight towers that would have given the city's defenders an unassailable advantage over enemy forces.

RIGHT: Behind Ávila's walls is a beautifully preserved city of Renaissance churches and palaces, such as the Santa Maria la Mayor shown here. The city has been designated a UNESCO World Heritage Site.

MERCADO TRADICIONAL DE LEON

PREVIOUS PAGE LEFT: Forty miles to the east of Valladolid is the striking Castillo Peñafiel. In this region of castles it stands out as one of the most impressive and also one of the most strategically important during the Reconquista.

PREVIOUS PAGE RIGHT: León was founded as a Roman encampment and over two thousand years has grown into a bustling city alive with reminders of its long history. The photograph shows Plaza Mayor on market day.

RIGHT: Outside of León, life goes on much as it has for centuries in small villages hidden in the hills and mountains.

FAR RIGHT: In northeastern Castilla y León is another Roman town: Astorga. Once an important staging post for Rome's legions, it is now noted for its relatively recent structures, the cathedral (built between the fifteenth and eighteenth centuries and seen here on the right) and the Palacio Episcopal (left), which dates to the nineteenth century.

LEFT: Houses and haystacks in León, at Herrerias de Valcarcel.

RIGHT: Mined for gold by the Romans over two centuries, Las Médulas in the province of León are a striking reminder of the ancient hydraulic technology that created the sheer cliff faces.

OVER PAGE LEFT: One of Spain's largest and most impressive squares is found in the city of Salamanca. It was built during the eighteenth century by order of Filipe V, whom the city loyally supported during the War of the Spanish Succession.

OVER PAGE RIGHT: The town of Béjar sits in the hills on the edge of Sierra de Gredos. Traditionally a textile manufacturing center, Béjar's sleepy ambience and mild climate make it a popular summer destination.

PREVIOUS PAGE LEFT: With its winding, arcaded streets, the town of Cáceres in the heart of Extremadura is redolent of its Renaissance heyday when its citizens included many wealthy merchants and aristocrats.

PREVIOUS PAGE RIGHT: Perched atop a hill, Trujillo is one of Extremadura's most scenic towns. Among its historic buildings is the Moorish fort that crowns the hill.

RIGHT: Trujillo's town square features a statue of conquistadore Francisco Pizarro, the conqueror of Peru. He was born in the town in 1475.

FAR RIGHT: Located in Extremadura's Badajoz province, Mérida was once the area's Roman capital. Of the many Roman remains that can be found around the town, the most important is the ancient theater, which is still used for performances.

Left: Also in the Badajoz province is the elegant little town of Zafra. Its neat streets are punctuated by picturesque squares watched over by a well-preserved Moorish fortress that now serves as a hotel.

Right: In the northern part of Castilla-La Mancha, the castle-dominated old town of Sigüenza clings to the side of a hill. Parts of the fortifications date back to the fifth century and were reinforced under the Moors two centuries later. Restored in the 1960s, the castle now serves as a hotel.

RIGHT: Belmonte castle in the province of Belmonte Cuenca in La Mancha was built on top of San Cristóbal hill by Juan Pacheco, Marquis of Villena between 1456-1470. It was abandoned in the nineteenth century but remains remarkably well preserved.

FOLLOWING PAGE LEFT: The plains of Campo da Criptana in Ciudad Real in central Spain are one of the hottest regions in the entire country.

FOLLOWING PAGE RIGHT: Typical of La Mancha are the pictuaresque windmills made famous by Miguel de Cervantes in his novel *Don Quixote*.

Infotur

Southern Spain

Schindler

Southern Spain

Across the bottom of Spain stretches one vast region: Andalusia. Fringed by the Atlantic Ocean to the west and the Mediterranean beyond the Straits of Gibraltar, the landscape here changes from arid deserts of Almería to the snow-capped mountains of the Sierra Nevada, and varies from wild hills to vineyards and olive groves. Andalusia is the region that most obviously reflects the popular perceptions of Spain. With its bullfighting rings, narrow streets of whitewashed houses, riotous festivals, rich cuisine, and seemingly endless beaches, it is perhaps Spain's most vibrant region, but also a place where the spirit of *mañana* (do it tomorrow) reigns. It was here that the art of flamenco originated, and the passionate, flamboyant dance perfectly captures the spirit of Andalusia.

The region is also home to some of Spain's most historically important cities. Seville, the capital, is a maze of cobbled alleyways and architectural gems. Granada and Córdoba are both redolent of the country's Moorish heritage. In fact, southern Spain was once the heart of Islamic Spain and reminders of the Moors are strewn across the landscape. Significant buildings include the Mezquita in the old Moorish capital of Córdoba, La Giralda tower and Real Alcázar in Seville, and—of course—the world-famous, and breathtakingly beautiful, Alhambra in Granada.

The grace with which the Moors designed their buildings has been influential ever since, and everywhere in Andalusia there are elegant arcaded squares and walled gardens where fountains cool the air.

Centuries before the Moors arrived, Andalusia was Roman Hispania Baetica, and the marks of the Roman Empire can also be found in abundance, especially at Itálica, which is among the best preserved Roman towns in Europe. The region also has picturesque whitewashed hilltop towns—fortified against bandit attacks in years past—and some of the finest Gothic architecture in Spain, including Seville's cathedral, where rest the remains of the region's most celebrated son, Christopher Columbus.

Noted for the pride its inhabitants take in the quality of their food and fortified wines—which are different from that produced in any other region and are served outdoors at atmospheric *bodegas* and *tapas* bars—Andalusia is a region of contrast and color where life revolves around enjoyment.

PREVIOUS PAGE: The island of La Cartuja was connected to the mainland for Seville's Expo '92. The exhibition's buildings still stand and the area remains a popular tourist attraction, not least for the theme park that has been constructed here.

RIGHT: Andalusia is the heartland of Moorish Spain and the Alcazaba fortress in Almería was the greatest of their fortifications. Dating to the end of the first millennium, it dominates the town, which in Moorish times was a major port.

LEFT: Away from Andalusia's beautiful coast is the Sierra Nevada range, where the highest peaks reach over 11,000 feet above sea level. A haven for wildlife, the range also provides the region with ski resorts throughout the winter.

RIGHT: The city of Granada is a beautifully situated jewel. With its irrigated gardens and peaceful courtyards, the Moorish influence on the city is easy to see.

OVER PAGE: Even in summer, patches of snow cling to the summits of the Sierra Nevada. The mountains are popular with hikers during the warmer months.

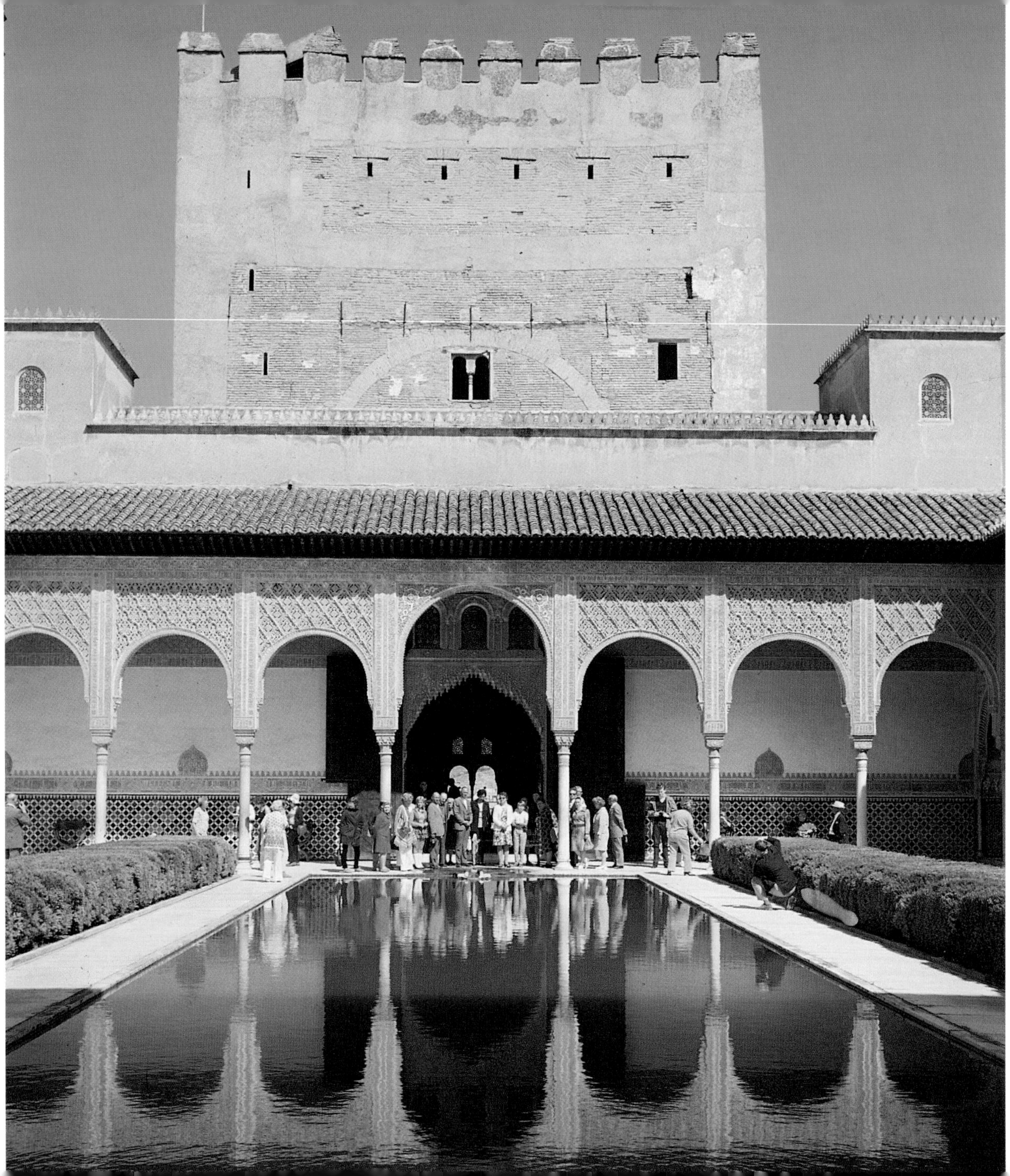

Left: Granada's most famous site is the Alhambra. Built during the final centuries of Moorish dominion over the region, the palace was intended to dazzle in order to reinforce the outside perception of the caliphs' power. This photograph shows the Patio Comares.

Right: The Alhambra's Patio Leones is an arcaded courtyard, richly embellished with Islamic ornamentation. At its center a fountain rests upon marble lions.

TURISMO

Previous page left: In the province of Jaen, sitting on a hill surrounded by olive groves, is the beautiful town of Baeza. Rich in Renaissance architecture, the entire town has been declared an historic site. Here in the Plaza del Populo stands the Roman fountain, Fuente de los Leones.

Previous page right: Baeza also boasts an imposing cathedral, built in 1567 by Andrés de Vandelvira. Standing in front of the cathedral is the Fuente de Santa Maria, a fountain designed by Ginés Martinez and finished in 1564.

Left: Úbeda was founded in 200 B.C. but its main points of interest are the many well-preserved Renaissance buildings found in the heart of the city. The most impressive example is the Plaza Vazquez with its sixteenth century palace and interior courtyard.

Right: The Castillo de Santa Catalina in Jaén was originally a hilltop fortress built by the Moors. The Moors named Jaén "Geen," which translates to "gateway for caravans"; not surprisingly, this was an important stop on the road between Castile and Andalusia.

Exposición
OLEOS
Y CERAS
Manolo
Fuertes
Del 14 al 26 de Junio
1 9 9 6

Far left: Malaga is famed for its many Moorish castillos and fortifications. Here is an example of a typical Moorish castle.

Left: The Iglesia del Sagrado Corazón in Malaga was constructed between 1907 and 1920 and is one of the most important works by architect Guerrero Strachan.

Left: A short walk form the centrer of Malaga are the fortified walls of Alcazaba, a fortress built between the eighth and eleventh centuries. The entrance through the walls is known as the Puerto del Cristo (port of Christ).

Right: The impressive eighth-century Moorish castle, Almodóvar del Rio, in Córdoba province, stands on a promontory overlooking cotton fields and the white-washed buildings of the town below.

Following page left: The Iglesia del Sagrario in Málaga. The city boasts many great cultural sights and achievements, not least that of being the birthplace of Pablo Picasso.

Following page right: The view over the port of Málaga shows how the Costa del Sol coast of Spain accommodates the old and the new side by side.

¿ ALMODÓVAR !
UTOPICA Y MESTIZA

PREVIOUS PAGE LEFT: Although there has been a fortification on this hill since Roman times, it was not until the Muslim occupation that the castle at Almodovar became the impressive stronghold that is seen today.

PREVIOUS PAGE RIGHT: Córdoba's Alcázar de los Reyes Cristianos was once the home of the great Catholic monarchs. Built during the fourteenth century, the palace's grounds are beautifully landscaped with pools and fountains.

LEFT: The Great Mosque in Córdoba, the Mezquita, is more than twelve centuries old. The original mosque was founded in 785 by Abd al Rahman I and many expansions were completed throughout the ensuing centuries.

RIGHT: The interior of the Mezquita has more than 850 arches and pillars. Made from a glittering mixture of granite, jasper, and marble, the building's effect is breathtaking.

PREVIOUS PAGE LEFT: In the Patio de los Naranjos orange trees grow among the palms. Part of the mosque was destroyed in 1523 in order to make room for a central cathedral.

PREVIOUS PAGE RIGHT: On its promontory at the southern border of Córdoba province at the edge of the Sierra Subeticas Natural Park, the town of Iznajar commands striking views of the man-made reservoir below.

RIGHT: Another view of the Mezquita in Córdoba.

FAR RIGHT: Away fom the bustle and noise of the main roads the back lanes and alleyways of Córdoba are typically Spanish—whitewashed buildings with decorative black grillwork, and brightly colored trailing geraniums.

RIGHT: Seville's Barrio de Danta Cruz is a particularly beautiful quarter of the picturesque city. Cobbled streets, old gardens, whitewashed houses, and excellent bars and restaurants make it popular with locals and tourists alike.

RIGHT: Located in the province of Seville and overlooking the rolling Sevillian plains, the town of Estepa has been inhabited by humans since prehistoric times and is an important archeological site.

LEFT: Designated a UNESCO World Heritage Site in 1987, the Archivo General de Indias in Seville is an outstanding example of Renaissance architecture. It houses historically important documents of the Spanish empire in the Americas and Philippines.

LEFT: One of the best ways to soak up Seville's historic atmosphere is by horse-drawn carriage.

Right: The bell tower known as La Giralda has stood in Seville for over 800 years. Built by the Moors in 1198, it was originally crowned with a minaret, which has been replaced with three successive designs, the latest in 1568.

Right: The twelve-sided Torre del Oro was originally a part of Seville's defense system. Built during the Almohad rule, a chain would have stretched beneath the Guadalquivir River to a similar structure on the opposite bank, preventing enemy ships from reaching the city's port.

PREVISION

LEFT: Built for the Spanish-American Exhibition of 1929, which was held in Seville, the Plaza de España was designed in the Moorish Revival style. Originally it housed the industrial exhibition; it is now a government building.

LEFT: Seville's cathedral holds the tomb of explorer Christopher Columbus, who planned his voyage to the Americas on nearby La Cartuja Island. In 2003 the tomb was opened and Columbus's bones subjected to DNA examination in order to settle an old dispute about his actual resting place. It was agreed that in all likelihood the remains were those of Columbus.

FAR LEFT: Transformed under Pedro I in the mid-fourteenth century, Seville's old Almohad palace became a stunning combination of Moorish and Spanish art and architecture.

LEFT: A few miles north of Seville is one of the country's most important archeological sites: the Roman town of Itálica. Founded in 206 B.C. by General Publius Cornelius Scipio, the remains include well-preserved mosaics, architecture, and an amphitheater.

Previous page left: Southeast of Seville, the city of Ronda is surely one of the most dramatically situated in the world. Perched atop rocky cliffs over a deep gorge, Ronda was once all but impregnable. In fact it was not until 1485 that the last Islamic troops were dislodged.

Previous page right: Jutting out into the Bay of Cádiz, the city is blessed by a number of beautiful beaches that are popular with vacationers, including la Caleta, shown here.

Right: The Andalusian town of Jerez de la Frontera is perhaps more famous for its sherry and brandy than its architecture. In fact, the Spanish word for "sherry" is "jerez." Nevertheless, the charming town is home to a magnificent, and unusual, cathedral that was originally built as a mosque by the Moors and has since been altered to reflect a number of different architectural styles.

Far right: The Palacio de Villavicenio in Jeréz was built on the ruins of an earlier Islamic castle. It was inherited by Bartholomew de Villavicencio in 1664; reconstruction of the fortress began shortly afterwards. The sensitively restored palace is also famous for its "Camera-Obscura," which is situated in the tower.

Far left: Jerez is famed for its equestrian expertise. Here in the Real Escuela Andaluza de Arte Ecuestre visitors can watch expert riders in dressage displays or see the horses being trained.

Left: Perhaps one of the most visually arresting churches in the province of Cadiz, La Cartuja de Jerez is famed for its intricate Greco-Roman façade and its small Gothic chapel.

Over page left: A colorful example of the impressive dressage displays available to visitors of the Real Escuela Andaluza de Arte Ecuestre in Jerez.

Over page right: The maritime town of Huelva is an ancient settlement on the Gulf of Cadiz. Christopher Columbus prepared for his first voyage of discovery here and in the process used local crews and resources and many local sights and attractions are devoted to the explorer.

RIGHT AND FAR RIGHT: The new and old faces of Almería. An ancient province on the southeastern coast of Andalucia, this is the driest area in Europe and also one of the warmest. In the second half of the twentieth century Almería became a major tourist destination and the local economy has never looked back.

Islands and Overseas Spain

Islands and Overseas Spain

Away from the mainland are two island chains that belong to Spain, the Balearics in the Mediterranean and the Canaries in the Atlantic. Both sets of islands are popular tourist destinations and as such, have garnered an unfortunate image of over crowded beaches, multi-story hotels and loud discotheques. Looking past this unfair image, visitors to the islands will find much more available and an unexpected idyll. The Balearic Islands include Ibiza, Formentera, Menorca, and Mallorca. The Canaries are La Palma, Tenerife, Gran Canaria, Fuerteventura, Lanzarote, and the tiny isles of El Hierro and La Gomera.

Ibiza is by far the most dynamic of the Balearics, with a world-renowned reputation for exciting night life and outrageous clubs and bars, as well as clear blue waters and clean sandy beaches. The largest of these islands, Mallorca has a spectacular natural landscape incorporating a wide variety of scenery, including lush plains, beautiful beaches, and lofty mountain ranges. Menorca lies further from the mainland than the rest of the Balearic islands and its isolation is obvious in many ways. The beaches here are less developed and the countryside unspoiled. In fact, Menorca has a large collection of ancient buildings, thought to date as far back as the Bronze Age.

Previous page: The second of Spain's two African territories is the town of Melilla, which was conquered in 1497. The enclave is a heady mix of Spanish and African cultures with a strong Muslim presence.

Right: The old town of Ibiza, also called "Dalt-Vila," is a winding, narrow maze of cobbled streets surrounded by towering ramparts. The entrance to Dalt-Vila is on top of a hill; the road then passes over a drawbridge and through the impressive Portal de Tablas, a gate bordered by Roman statues.

The Canary Islands, lying off the coast of Morocco, were formed from erupting volcanoes more than fourteen million years ago and their volcanic origins are still visible today. Tenerife has the stunning National Park of Mount Teide, which features the remnants of a huge dormant volcano and the lava-scarred landscape surrounding its base. The beaches of Tenerife are coated in black sand, another vestige of volcanic activity. The tiny islands of La Palma, El Hierro, and La Gomera are famous for being the last stops of Christopher Columbus before he set out on his voyages across the globe, but they have little to offer tourists apart from unspoiled countryside.

La Palma is dominated by the huge volcanic crater, La Caldera de Taburiente. The large erosion crater is more than five miles wide and surrounded by a protected National Park. Gran Canaria, Lanzarote, and Fuerteventura have been popular tourist destinations for decades, all offering long clean beaches, sunshine, and beautiful countryside, yet at the same time each island has retained its own unique identity.

The last stops on this photographic tour of Spain are the last tiny remnants of its empire in Africa, the towns of Cueta and Melilla. These fortified towns have a rich heritage all their own. Here Africa mingles with Spain to create a vibrant mixture.

Left: Always a popular destination for vacationers, Ibiza possesses many fine beaches. Here at Cala San Vicente, families can enjoy the sea, protected by the curve of the bay and the warm, shallow waters.

Left: The busy port of Ibiza is a popular place for sailing or to rent a boat—or for the rich and famous to simply moor their yachts.

RIGHT AND FAR RIGHT: Ibiza is a major Mediterranean tourist destination with people flocking to the island to enjoy the wonderful climate and fantastic food, as well as all the many and varied beaches, bars, clubs, and restauants.

RIGHT: Dominating the views over both the town and the waterfront, Palma's golden cathedral is a dramatic sight. Legend has it that when Jaime I of Aragon found himself in fear for his life when caught in a squall at sea, he promised God that he would build a great church if he survived.

OVER PAGE: Another view of Palma's great Gothic cathedal. Construction started in 1230, but was not completed until 1601, well over three hundred years later.

PEVIOUS PAGE LEFT: Son Corro is a megalithic settlement in the center of the island between Costitx and Sencelles, Mallorca. Three extraordinary ancient life-size bronze bulls heads were found at this site and are now on display in the National Archaeological Museum in Madrid.

PREVIOUS RIGHT: One of the many defensive watchtowers placed around Ibiza's coastline, the Torre del Pirata was built to warn the inhabitants of approaching pirates who were renowned for ransacking the islands towns and villages

LEFT: Palma's Gothic Castell de Bellver was originally commissioned by Jamie II of Aragon as a summer residence, but it soon became a prison and remained one until 1915.

RIGHT: The turquoise waters, white sands, and dazzlingly impressive marina of Cala'n Bosch on the southwestern coast of Menorca have made it one of the most popular tourist destinations of the islands.

HOTEL CALA'N BOSCH
MARINA
Tapinet
7ª-MH-2-462

RIGHT: Another view of Mount Teide, the third largest volcano on Tenerife. It is classed as being currently dormant and last erupted in 1909, although minor emissions show that another eruption is likley.

FAR RIGHT: *Spartocytisus supranubius* is a Canary island native plant that thrives at higher altitudes. It is shown flowering and growing in front of another distinctive native plant, Canary Pines (*Pinus canariensis*), on Tenerife in Teide Volcano National Park.

PREVIOUS PAGE LEFT AND RIGHT: At 12,198 feet high, El Teide is Spain's highest mountain and is still classed as an active volcano. Set within a national park of the same name, the surrounding landscape is littered with volcanic debris and amazing rock formations.

RIGHT: Close to the village of Cueva del Polvo are Tenerife's famous Los Gigantes cliffs. Formed by volcanic activity and shaped by the Atlantic, "the giants" are a spectacular destination for beach lovers.

FAR RIGHT: The village of Los Realejos, situated on the northern side of Tenerife close to the Orotava Valley, is surrounded by natural beauty. Almost half of the village is protected by strict environmental laws.

FAR LEFT: The Dragon trees—*Dracaena draco*—are indigenous to the Canaries and according to legend were originally dragons. These large intriguing trees are impossible to date, but are definately a number of centuries old.

LEFT: The cathedral of San Cristóbal de la Laguna on Tenerife

PREVIOUS PAGE LEFT: La Orotava lies on the northern coast of Tenerife at the end of a lush valley of parks and banana plantations. Distinguished by its flamboyant architecture and shady squares, the town also boasts botanical gardens and volcanic dark sand beaches.

PREVIOUS PAGE RIGHT: On the northwest coast of the island, Puerto de Garachico was completely buried by a volcanic eruption in 1706. Since then it has been rebuilt into one of the islands most beautiful villages.

RIGHT: A few miles from Santa Cruz de Tenerife is one of the island's most popular beaches. Las Teresitas is, in fact, formed from sand brought here from the Sahara.

FAR RIGHT: The capital city of Tenerife—Santa Cruz—is also its busiest port, welcoming commercial shipping and pleasure cruises from around the world as it has for centuries.

Left: At the heart of Santa Cruz de Tenerife is a lovely old square, the Plaza de España. Close to the harbor, it is lined by tranquil churches.

Right: Santa Cruz is an eclectic mix of historic and modern buildings. It also has an excellent art museum, the Museo de Bellas Artes, as well as parks lined with modern sculpture and a lively African market.

LEFT: Away from Gran Canaria's beaches are caves that have been inhabited for thousands of years. Archeologists believe that the Canary Islands' first inhabitants migrated here from North Africa.

RIGHT: Formed by a volcanic eruption Roque Nublo (meaning "Rock Clouded"), is an imposing natural 250-foot monolith standing over the town of Tajeda on Gran Canaria.

Right: The imposing cathedral of Santa Ana in Las Palmas de Gran Canaria is designed in a style known as Atlantic Gothic and is an amalgamation of different architectural styles. This is because it took over three hundred and fifty years to build starting in the early fifteenth century.

Over page left: Containing more than 1,000 species of cacti, Lanzarote's Jardín de Cactus was designed by local artist Cesar Manrique and is perfectly set amid volcanic rocks.

Over page right: Perhaps Lanzarote's most awe-inspiring sight is the Montañas de Fuego in the Timanfaya National Park. The barren volcanic landscape is a protected UNESCO Biosphere Reserve.

PREVIOUS PAGES: Once an important commercial Mediterranean port and a surprisingly dynamic center of the Art Nouveau and Modernist movements, Melilla is now primarily a fishing port.

ABOVE: A Spanish enclave since it was taken from Portugal in 1668, Ceuta lies on the North African coast on the Straits of Gibraltar. The town's strategic importance is underlined in the severe fortress that has stood here since the fourteenth century.

RIGHT: Melilla was a Berber town on the North African coast until it was conquered by the Spanish in 1497. In its time it has been Phoenician, Punic, Roman, Byzantine, Vandal, Visigothic, Muslim, and then finally, a Christian Spanish possession. It is currently a Spanish exclave on the Mediterranean Rif coast of Morocco.